Mastering the CCNA: A Comprehensive Exam Prep Guide

Table of Contents

Chapter 1: Introduction to CCNA Certification

Chapter 2: Networking Fundamentals

Chapter 3: IP Addressing and Subnetting

Chapter 4: Routing and Switching

Chapter 5: Network Services and Security

Chapter 6: WAN Technologies

Chapter 7: Network Management and Troubleshooting

Chapter 8: Wireless Technologies

Chapter 9: Network Automation and Programmability

Chapter 10: Network Virtualization and Software-Defined Infrastructure

Chapter 11: Network Design Principles and Best Practices

Chapter 12: Network Troubleshooting Techniques and Methodologies

Chapter 13: Network Monitoring and Performance Optimization

Chapter 14: Network Security Best Practices

Chapter 1: Introduction to CCNA Certification

In this chapter, we will provide you with an overview of the Cisco Certified Network Associate (CCNA) certification. We'll explore the benefits of obtaining this certification, understand the exam structure and requirements, and help you kickstart your CCNA exam preparation journey.

Section 1: Understanding CCNA Certification

Welcome to the world of CCNA! The CCNA certification is a widely recognized credential in the IT industry, demonstrating your expertise in networking fundamentals, routing and switching technologies, network security, and more. It serves as a solid foundation for a successful career in networking.

To achieve CCNA certification, you must pass a comprehensive exam that tests your knowledge and skills related to Cisco networking technologies. The exam covers various topics, including network fundamentals, IP addressing and subnetting, routing and switching concepts, network services and security, WAN technologies, wireless technologies, and network troubleshooting.

Section 2: Benefits of CCNA Certification

Earning the CCNA certification offers several benefits, both personally and professionally. Here are a few key advantages:

Enhanced Career Opportunities: CCNA certification opens up a wide range of career opportunities in the networking field. Employers often prefer candidates with industry-recognized certifications, and CCNA can help you stand out from the competition.

Expanded Knowledge and Skills: The CCNA curriculum provides a comprehensive understanding of networking technologies, protocols, and best practices. It equips you with the skills needed to design, configure, and troubleshoot networks effectively.

Networking Community and Resources: As a CCNA-certified professional, you gain access to a vibrant community of networking experts. You can connect with other CCNA-certified individuals, participate in forums, and access valuable resources and study materials.

Section 3: CCNA Exam Structure and Requirements

Now, let's dive into the details of the CCNA exam structure and requirements. Here's what you need to know:

Exam Format: The CCNA exam consists of multiple-choice questions, drag-and-drop activities, simulations, and simlets. It is a proctored exam, typically administered at Pearson VUE testing centers or online.

Exam Duration: The exam duration is typically 120 minutes (2 hours), although it may vary depending on the version of the exam.

Passing Score: Cisco does not disclose the exact passing score for the CCNA exam. The passing score is determined based on a scaled score system, taking into account the difficulty level of the questions.

Exam Registration: To register for the CCNA exam, visit the official Cisco certification website or Pearson VUE website. Follow the registration process, pay the exam fee, and schedule your exam date and location.

Section 4: Getting Started with CCNA Exam Preparation

Preparing for the CCNA exam requires dedication, practice, and a structured approach. Here are a few steps to get you started:

Review the Exam Blueprint: Familiarize yourself with the CCNA exam blueprint, which outlines the topics and subtopics covered in the exam. This will serve as a roadmap for your study plan.

Gather Study Materials: Invest in reliable study materials, such as official Cisco books, online courses, video tutorials, and practice exams. These resources will help you gain a deeper understanding of the exam topics and provide opportunities for hands-on practice.

Create a Study Plan: Develop a study plan that suits your schedule and learning style. Allocate dedicated time for each exam topic, ensuring you cover all the essential areas before your exam date.

Hands-On Practice: Networking is a practical field, so hands-on practice is crucial. Set up a lab environment using network simulators or physical equipment to gain practical experience in configuring and troubleshooting networks.

Join Study Groups or Forums: Engage with other CCNA aspirants by joining study groups or online forums. Discussing concepts, sharing study resources, and clarifying doubts with peers can enhance your learning experience.

Take Practice Exams: Regularly attempt practice exams to evaluate your knowledge and identify areas that require further attention. Practice exams also help you become familiar with the exam format and time management.

Remember, CCNA certification is attainable with proper dedication and consistent effort. As you progress through this book, we will delve deeper into each exam topic, providing detailed explanations, examples, and hands-on exercises to reinforce your understanding.

Congratulations on taking the first step towards becoming a Cisco Certified Network Associate! With determination and the right resources, you'll be well on your way to mastering the CCNA exam.

Chapter 2: Networking Fundamentals

Section 1: Introduction to Computer Networks

Welcome to Chapter 2 of our CCNA Exam Prep book! In this chapter, we will explore the fundamental concepts of computer networks. Understanding these concepts is crucial for building a strong foundation in networking. Let's get started!

A computer network is a collection of interconnected devices that can communicate and share resources with each other. Networks can range from small local networks within a home or office to large-scale networks connecting geographically dispersed locations.

Section 2: OSI and TCP/IP Models

To facilitate communication between devices in a network, we use a set of protocols and standards. Two widely adopted models for conceptualizing network protocols are the Open Systems Interconnection (OSI) model and the TCP/IP model.

OSI Model:

The OSI model is a conceptual framework that defines how network protocols interact and function. It consists of seven layers:

Physical Layer: This layer deals with the physical transmission of data over the network medium, such as cables or wireless signals.

Data Link Layer: The data link layer ensures reliable transmission of data between directly connected devices. It handles error detection and correction.

Network Layer: The network layer focuses on logical addressing and routing of data packets across different networks.

Transport Layer: The transport layer provides end-to-end communication between devices. It ensures data reliability, flow control, and error recovery.

Session Layer: The session layer establishes, maintains, and terminates connections between devices, enabling communication sessions.

Presentation Layer: This layer deals with data formatting, encryption, and compression, ensuring that data is presented correctly.

Application Layer: The application layer is where user applications interact with the network. It includes protocols such as HTTP, FTP, and SMTP.

TCP/IP Model:

The TCP/IP model is a simpler, four-layered model widely used in modern networking. The layers are as follows:

Network Interface Layer: This layer corresponds to the combined functionality of the physical and data link layers in the OSI model.

Internet Layer: Similar to the network layer in the OSI model, the internet layer handles IP addressing, routing, and packet fragmentation.

Transport Layer: This layer is equivalent to the transport layer in the OSI model and provides reliable end-to-end data delivery.

Application Layer: The application layer in the TCP/IP model encompasses the functionality of the session, presentation, and application layers in the OSI model.

Section 3: Network Protocols and Topologies

Network Protocols:

Network protocols define the rules and formats for communication between devices in a network. Some commonly used protocols include:

Internet Protocol (IP): IP is responsible for logical addressing and routing of packets across networks.

Transmission Control Protocol (TCP): TCP provides reliable, connection-oriented communication between devices.

User Datagram Protocol (UDP): UDP is a connectionless, unreliable protocol used for fast transmission of data.

Internet Control Message Protocol (ICMP): ICMP is used for diagnostic and error-reporting purposes, such as ping and traceroute.

Network Topologies:

Network topology refers to the physical or logical arrangement of devices in a network. Some common network topologies are:

Bus Topology: Devices are connected in a linear bus, with a shared communication medium.

Star Topology: Devices are connected to a central hub or switch.

Ring Topology: Devices form a closed loop, where each device is connected to its adjacent neighbors.

Mesh Topology: Each device is directly connected to every other device in the network.

Understanding different network topologies helps in designing and troubleshooting networks effectively.

Section 4: Ethernet and LAN Technologies

Ethernet is a widely used technology for local area networks (LANs). It defines the standards for physical connections and data transmission over LANs. Some key concepts related to Ethernet and LAN technologies include:

Ethernet Frames: Ethernet frames encapsulate data for transmission over the network. They consist of source and destination MAC addresses, data payload, and other control information.

Ethernet Switching: Ethernet switches connect multiple devices in a LAN, enabling efficient and secure communication. They use MAC addresses to forward frames to the correct destination device.

LAN Technologies: LAN technologies, such as Ethernet, can operate at different speeds, including 10 Mbps, 100 Mbps, 1 Gbps, and higher. The choice of LAN technology depends on the network requirements and available infrastructure.

Understanding Ethernet and LAN technologies is essential for configuring and troubleshooting LAN environments.

Congratulations on completing Chapter 2! In this chapter, you learned about the fundamental concepts of computer networks, including the OSI and TCP/IP models, network protocols, and network topologies. Additionally, you explored Ethernet and LAN technologies commonly used in local area networks. This knowledge forms a strong foundation for your CCNA exam preparation. In the next chapter, we will delve into IP addressing and subnetting, an essential topic for network configuration.

Chapter 3: IP Addressing and Subnetting

Section 1: Introduction to IP Addressing

Welcome to Chapter 3 of our CCNA Exam Prep book! In this chapter, we will dive into the world of IP addressing and subnetting. IP addressing is a fundamental concept in networking, and understanding it is crucial for designing and configuring networks. Let's get started!

An IP address is a unique numerical identifier assigned to each device connected to a network. It allows devices to communicate with each other over an IP-based network, such as the Internet. IP addresses come in two versions: IPv4 and IPv6. We'll focus on IPv4, as it is still widely used.

IPv4 addresses consist of four octets (32 bits) expressed in decimal format. Each octet can range from 0 to 255, representing a total of approximately 4.3 billion unique IP addresses.

Section 2: IP Address Classes

IPv4 addresses are divided into classes, which help determine the network and host portions of an IP address. The five classes are:

Class A: The first octet represents the network portion, and the remaining three octets represent the host portion. Class A addresses are used for large networks.

Class B: The first two octets represent the network portion, and the remaining two octets represent the host portion. Class B addresses are used for medium-sized networks.

Class C: The first three octets represent the network portion, and the last octet represents the host portion. Class C addresses are used for small networks.

Class D: Class D addresses are reserved for multicast addresses, which allow efficient one-to-many communication.

Class E: Class E addresses are reserved for experimental or research purposes.

Understanding IP address classes helps in network planning and addressing assignments.

Section 3: Subnetting Concepts and Calculations

Subnetting allows us to divide a large network into smaller subnetworks or subnets. It provides flexibility in managing IP addresses and enhances network efficiency. Let's explore the key concepts and calculations involved in subnetting.

Subnet Mask:

A subnet mask is a 32-bit value used to determine the network and host portions of an IP address. It works by applying a logical AND operation between the IP address and the subnet mask. The result helps identify the network to which the IP address belongs.

Subnet masks are represented using dotted decimal notation, just like IP addresses. The bits set to 1 in the subnet mask represent the network portion, and the bits set to 0 represent the host portion.

Subnetting Calculation:

To perform subnetting, you need to determine the number of subnets and hosts required. This information helps in selecting an appropriate subnet mask and allocating IP addresses.

The subnetting calculation involves the following steps:

Determine the number of required subnets: This depends on the network's design and the number of separate subnetworks needed.

Determine the number of required hosts per subnet: Consider the number of devices that will be connected to each subnet.

Choose an appropriate subnet mask: Based on the number of subnets and hosts, select a subnet mask that provides the required number of network and host bits.

Section 4: Variable Length Subnet Masking (VLSM)

Variable Length Subnet Masking (VLSM) is a technique that allows subnetting with different-sized subnets within the same network. It enables efficient utilization of IP addresses and improves network scalability.

With VLSM, you can allocate smaller subnets to network segments that require more IP addresses while assigning larger subnets to segments with fewer devices. This flexibility optimizes IP address allocation and conserves address space.

Section 5: IPv6 Addressing

As the world transitions to IPv6 due to the exhaustion of IPv4 addresses, understanding IPv6 addressing becomes crucial. IPv6 addresses are 128 bits long, written in hexadecimal format, and are separated by colons. They provide an enormous address space and improved features compared to IPv4.

IPv6 addresses employ a hierarchical addressing structure, consisting of a network prefix and an interface identifier. The network prefix identifies the network portion, and the interface identifier identifies the host portion.

Congratulations on completing Chapter 3! In this chapter, you learned about IP addressing, including address classes, subnetting concepts and calculations, and Variable Length Subnet Masking (VLSM). You also gained an introduction to IPv6 addressing. This knowledge is essential for network planning, configuration, and troubleshooting. In the next chapter, we will explore routing and switching concepts, which form the backbone of network communication.

Chapter 4: Routing and Switching

Section 1: Introduction to Routing and Switching

Welcome to Chapter 4 of our CCNA Exam Prep book! In this chapter, we will delve into routing and switching concepts, which are essential for effective network communication. Routing involves forwarding data packets between networks, while switching facilitates communication within a local network. Let's explore these concepts in detail!

Section 2: Routing Concepts and Protocols

Routing plays a critical role in connecting networks and enabling data transfer. Here are some key concepts related to routing:

Router:

A router is a network device that forwards data packets between different networks based on their destination IP addresses. Routers examine the IP headers of incoming packets to determine the optimal path for forwarding.

Routing Table:

A routing table is a data structure maintained by routers that contains information about the available networks and the paths to reach them. It includes entries with destination network addresses and corresponding next-hop addresses.

Routing Protocols:

Routing protocols enable routers to exchange information and build routing tables dynamically. Common routing protocols include:

Routing Information Protocol (RIP): A distance-vector routing protocol that uses hop count as a metric.

Open Shortest Path First (OSPF): A link-state routing protocol that calculates the shortest path to a destination using metrics such as bandwidth and delay.

Enhanced Interior Gateway Routing Protocol (EIGRP): A Cisco proprietary routing protocol that combines characteristics of both distance-vector and link-state protocols.

Understanding routing concepts and protocols is crucial for configuring and troubleshooting networks.

Section 3: Switching Concepts and Technologies

Switching facilitates communication within a local network by forwarding data frames between connected devices. Let's explore some key switching concepts and technologies:

Switch:

A switch is a network device that connects multiple devices in a local area network (LAN). It operates at the data link layer (Layer 2) of the OSI model and uses MAC addresses to forward data frames to the appropriate destination devices.

VLAN (Virtual Local Area Network):

VLANs divide a physical LAN into multiple logical segments, allowing devices to be grouped together virtually. VLANs provide improved security, broadcast control, and flexibility in network design.

Spanning Tree Protocol (STP):

STP is a protocol that prevents loops in switched networks by creating a loop-free logical topology. It ensures that only one path is active at a time between any two devices, providing redundancy and avoiding broadcast storms.

EtherChannel:

EtherChannel, also known as link aggregation, allows multiple physical links between switches to be combined into a single logical link. This increases bandwidth, provides load balancing, and enhances link redundancy.

Understanding switching concepts and technologies is crucial for designing and managing local networks effectively.

Section 4: Inter-VLAN Routing

Inter-VLAN routing enables communication between devices in different VLANs. By default, devices within a VLAN can communicate with each other, but communication between devices in different VLANs requires a router or a layer 3 switch.

Inter-VLAN routing can be achieved through the following methods:

Router-on-a-Stick: A single physical interface on a router is used to connect to a switch, and subinterfaces are configured for each VLAN.

Layer 3 Switch: A layer 3 switch has built-in routing capabilities and can perform inter-VLAN routing without the need for a separate router.

Section 5: Routing and Switching Configuration and Troubleshooting

To configure and troubleshoot routing and switching, you need to be familiar with various commands and tools. Some common configuration and troubleshooting tasks include:

Configuring IP addresses and routing protocols on routers

Configuring VLANs, trunking, and inter-VLAN routing on switches

Verifying routing and switching configurations using command-line interfaces (CLIs) and graphical user interfaces (GUIs)

Troubleshooting connectivity issues, routing errors, and switch configuration problems

Hands-on practice and familiarity with command-line tools, such as Cisco IOS commands, are crucial for mastering routing and switching configuration and troubleshooting.

Congratulations on completing Chapter 4! In this chapter, you learned about routing and switching concepts, including routers, routing tables, routing protocols, switches, VLANs, STP, EtherChannel, inter-VLAN routing, and configuration and troubleshooting techniques. These concepts are fundamental for building and managing networks. In the next chapter, we will explore network services and security, vital aspects of a robust and secure network infrastructure.

Chapter 5: Network Services and Security

Section 1: Introduction to Network Services

Welcome to Chapter 5 of our CCNA Exam Prep book! In this chapter, we will explore network services and security, two crucial aspects of network infrastructure. Network services provide various functionalities, while network security ensures the protection of data and resources. Let's dive in!

Section 2: DHCP (Dynamic Host Configuration Protocol)

DHCP, or Dynamic Host Configuration Protocol, is a network service that automatically assigns IP addresses and other network configuration parameters to devices. Here's what you need to know about DHCP:

DHCP Server:

A DHCP server is responsible for managing IP address pools and lease durations. When a device connects to a network, it can send a DHCP request to obtain an IP address and other configuration details from the DHCP server.

DHCP Lease:

When a device acquires an IP address through DHCP, it is leased for a specific duration. Before the lease expires, the device can renew or release the IP address. If the lease is not renewed, the IP address is returned to the DHCP server's pool for reassignment.

Understanding DHCP is essential for automating IP address assignments and managing network resources effectively.

Section 3: DNS (Domain Name System)

DNS, or Domain Name System, is a network service that translates domain names into IP addresses. It provides the mapping between human-readable domain names (e.g., www.example.com) and their corresponding IP addresses. Here's what you need to know about DNS:

DNS Resolution:

When a user enters a domain name in a web browser, the DNS resolution process begins. The DNS resolver on the user's device sends a DNS query to a DNS server to obtain the IP address associated with the domain name.

DNS Hierarchy:

The DNS system is hierarchical, with multiple levels of DNS servers. The root DNS servers handle top-level domains (TLDs), such as .com or .org. Authoritative DNS servers manage specific domain zones and provide IP address mappings for domain names.

Understanding DNS is crucial for navigating the Internet and ensuring proper communication between devices using domain names.

Section 4: NAT (Network Address Translation)

NAT, or Network Address Translation, is a network service used to translate private IP addresses to public IP addresses and vice versa. It allows multiple devices on a private network to share a single public IP address. Here's what you need to know about NAT:

Private and Public IP Addresses:

Private IP addresses are reserved for use within private networks and are not routable over the Internet. Public IP addresses are globally unique and can be used for communication over the Internet.

NAT Types:

Static NAT: A one-to-one mapping between private and public IP addresses, allowing direct communication with a specific device.

Dynamic NAT: A pool of public IP addresses is used to map to private IP addresses dynamically.

Port Address Translation (PAT): Also known as NAT overload, PAT maps multiple private IP addresses to a single public IP address using different port numbers.

Understanding NAT is crucial for conserving public IP address space and enabling communication between private and public networks.

Section 5: ACLs (Access Control Lists)

ACLs, or Access Control Lists, are security features used to control network traffic and protect resources. They can be configured on routers or switches to filter traffic based on source or destination IP addresses, ports, or other criteria. Here's what you need to know about ACLs:

Standard ACLs:

Standard ACLs filter traffic based on source IP addresses only. They are commonly used to control access to network resources based on specific source addresses or subnets.

Extended ACLs:

Extended ACLs filter traffic based on source and destination IP addresses, ports, and other criteria. They offer more granular control and are commonly used for complex access control requirements.

Understanding ACLs is essential for implementing network security policies and restricting unauthorized access to resources.

Section 6: Basic Network Security Principles

Network security is a critical aspect of any network infrastructure. Here are some fundamental principles to consider:

Confidentiality:

Protecting sensitive data from unauthorized access or disclosure by using encryption, access controls, and secure communication protocols.

Integrity:

Ensuring that data remains intact and unaltered during transmission or storage. Techniques like checksums and digital signatures help maintain data integrity.

Availability:

Ensuring that network resources and services are available to authorized users when needed. This involves implementing redundancy, fault tolerance, and appropriate security measures.

Authentication and Authorization:

Verifying the identity of users and devices to ensure authorized access to resources. Authentication mechanisms such as passwords, certificates, or biometrics are commonly used.

Network Monitoring:

Implementing tools and techniques to monitor network traffic, detect anomalies, and respond to security incidents promptly.

Understanding these basic security principles is crucial for designing secure network architectures and implementing effective security measures.

Congratulations on completing Chapter 5! In this chapter, you learned about network services such as DHCP, DNS, and NAT, which provide essential functionalities for network communication. You also explored ACLs, a security feature used to control traffic, and basic network security principles. This knowledge will help you design and secure networks effectively. In the next chapter, we will dive into WAN (Wide Area Network) technologies, expanding our understanding of network connectivity over larger distances.

Chapter 6: WAN Technologies

Section 1: Introduction to Wide Area Networks (WANs)

Welcome to Chapter 6 of our CCNA Exam Prep book! In this chapter, we will explore Wide Area Networks (WANs), which connect geographically dispersed locations. WAN technologies enable communication over large distances and play a crucial role in network connectivity. Let's dive into the world of WANs!

Section 2: Leased Lines

Leased lines are dedicated communication lines between two locations, providing constant, high-quality connectivity. Here's what you need to know about leased lines:

T1/E1 and T3/E3:

T1/E1 and T3/E3 lines are commonly used leased lines. T1 lines operate at 1.544 Mbps, while T3 lines operate at 45 Mbps. E1 and E3 lines are their European equivalents.

Point-to-Point Protocol (PPP):

PPP is a data link protocol commonly used over leased lines. It provides authentication, data encapsulation, and error detection capabilities, ensuring reliable communication between devices.

High-Level Data Link Control (HDLC):

HDLC is a synchronous data link protocol used by Cisco devices. It is similar to PPP and is commonly used in leased line connections.

Section 3: MPLS (Multiprotocol Label Switching)

MPLS is a packet-switched network technology used to transport data over WANs efficiently. It provides fast and reliable communication by assigning labels to packets, enabling streamlined forwarding. Here's what you need to know about MPLS:

Label Switching Routers (LSRs):

LSRs are devices that participate in MPLS networks. They examine labels attached to incoming packets and forward them based on the label information.

Label Distribution Protocol (LDP):

LDP is a protocol used by LSRs to exchange label information and build forwarding tables. It ensures consistent label assignment across the MPLS network.

MPLS VPN:

MPLS VPNs provide secure connectivity between geographically dispersed locations. They enable the creation of virtual private networks over a shared MPLS infrastructure, ensuring data privacy and isolation.

Section 4: VPN (Virtual Private Network)

VPNs allow secure communication over public networks by establishing encrypted tunnels. Here's what you need to know about VPNs:

Site-to-Site VPN:

A site-to-site VPN connects multiple locations, such as branch offices, over the public Internet. It enables secure communication by encrypting traffic between sites.

Remote Access VPN:

A remote access VPN allows individual users to connect securely to a private network from remote locations. It provides encrypted access to resources over the Internet.

VPN Protocols:

Common VPN protocols include IPsec (Internet Protocol Security), SSL/TLS (Secure Sockets Layer/Transport Layer Security), and OpenVPN. Each protocol has its strengths and is suitable for different use cases.

Section 5: WAN Connectivity Options

Various WAN connectivity options are available to meet different networking requirements. Let's explore a few common options:

Digital Subscriber Line (DSL):

DSL provides high-speed internet access over existing copper telephone lines. It offers faster speeds compared to traditional dial-up connections.

Cable Internet:

Cable internet utilizes cable television infrastructure to provide high-speed connectivity. It offers higher bandwidth than DSL but shares network resources with other users in the same area.

Fiber Optic:

Fiber optic connections use light signals transmitted through thin glass fibers to provide high-speed and reliable connectivity. They offer superior speed and bandwidth compared to traditional copper-based connections.

Wireless WAN:

Wireless WAN technologies, such as 4G/5G cellular networks, provide connectivity without the need for physical cables. They are useful in remote areas or as backup connections.

Understanding WAN connectivity options helps in selecting the most appropriate solution based on location, bandwidth requirements, and budget.

Congratulations on completing Chapter 6! In this chapter, you learned about WAN technologies, including leased lines, MPLS, VPNs, and various connectivity options. These technologies enable reliable and secure communication over large distances. In the next chapter, we will focus on network management and troubleshooting, equipping you with the skills to monitor and maintain network performance.

Chapter 7: Network Management and Troubleshooting

Section 1: Introduction to Network Management

Welcome to Chapter 7 of our CCNA Exam Prep book! In this chapter, we will explore network management and troubleshooting, essential skills for maintaining and optimizing network performance. Effective network management ensures smooth operation and helps identify and resolve issues promptly. Let's dive into the world of network management!

Section 2: SNMP (Simple Network Management Protocol)

SNMP, or Simple Network Management Protocol, is a widely used network management protocol. It allows network administrators to monitor and manage network devices, collect performance data, and receive alerts about potential issues. Here's what you need to know about SNMP:

SNMP Components:

Managed Devices: These are network devices, such as routers, switches, and servers, that support SNMP and can be monitored and managed.

SNMP Manager: The SNMP manager is the network management system that collects and analyzes data from managed devices.

SNMP Agents: SNMP agents reside on managed devices and collect and send data to the SNMP manager.

SNMP Versions:

SNMP has multiple versions, including SNMPv1, SNMPv2c, and SNMPv3. Each version provides different capabilities and security features.

MIB (Management Information Base):

MIB is a database that defines the structure and attributes of managed objects within SNMP-enabled devices. It provides a standardized way to access and manage device-specific information.

Section 3: Network Monitoring and Troubleshooting Tools

Network monitoring and troubleshooting tools help identify and resolve network issues efficiently. Here are some common tools used for network management:

Ping and Traceroute:

Ping is a utility that sends an ICMP Echo Request to a destination IP address to check if it is reachable. Traceroute is a tool that traces the path packets take to reach a destination, showing each hop along the way.

Network Analyzers:

Network analyzers, also known as packet sniffers, capture and analyze network traffic. They help identify network performance issues, troubleshoot network protocols, and detect security threats.

Syslog:

Syslog is a standard protocol used to collect and forward system log messages from various network devices. Centralized logging and analysis of syslog messages assist in troubleshooting and monitoring network events.

SNMP Monitoring Tools:

There are numerous SNMP monitoring tools available that simplify the management and monitoring of SNMP-enabled devices. These tools provide real-time monitoring, data visualization, and alerting capabilities.

Section 4: Common Network Issues and Troubleshooting

Network issues can arise due to various factors, including misconfigurations, connectivity problems, or hardware failures. Here are some common network issues and troubleshooting techniques:

Connectivity Issues:

Physical Layer: Check cables, connectors, and physical connections for any faults or damages.

Configuration Issues: Verify device configurations, including IP addresses, subnet masks, and default gateways.

Network Addressing: Ensure correct IP addressing, subnetting, and DHCP configurations.

Slow Network Performance:

Bandwidth Bottlenecks: Identify devices or links causing high network utilization and congestion.

Quality of Service (QoS): Implement QoS policies to prioritize critical traffic and improve network performance.

Network Protocol Issues: Analyze network protocols for any misconfigurations or compatibility issues.

Security Incidents:

Intrusion Detection Systems (IDS) and Intrusion Prevention Systems (IPS): Implement IDS and IPS solutions to detect and prevent unauthorized access and attacks.

Firewall Configurations: Verify firewall rules and configurations to ensure proper security measures.

Understanding common network issues and troubleshooting techniques is crucial for maintaining a stable and secure network environment.

Section 5: Network Documentation and Best Practices

Network documentation is an important aspect of network management. It helps ensure proper configuration, troubleshooting, and maintenance of the network. Here are some best practices for network documentation:

Network Diagrams:

Create detailed network diagrams that illustrate the network topology, device connections, and IP addressing schemes.

These diagrams provide a visual representation of the network infrastructure.

Configuration Backups:

Regularly back up device configurations to ensure quick restoration in case of device failures or misconfigurations.

Change Management:

Implement a change management process to track and document network changes, ensuring proper planning, testing, and approval before making any modifications.

Standard Operating Procedures (SOPs):

Develop and maintain SOPs that outline common network management and troubleshooting procedures. These documents provide step-by-step instructions for handling routine tasks and resolving issues.

By following proper network documentation and best practices, you can streamline network management and ensure efficient troubleshooting.

Congratulations on completing Chapter 7! In this chapter, you learned about network management and troubleshooting, including SNMP, network monitoring tools, common network issues, and documentation best practices. These skills are essential for maintaining network performance and resolving issues promptly. In the next chapter, we will explore wireless technologies, an increasingly important aspect of modern networking.

Chapter 8: Wireless Technologies

Section 1: Introduction to Wireless Technologies

Welcome to Chapter 8 of our CCNA Exam Prep book! In this chapter, we will explore wireless technologies, which have become integral to modern networking. Wireless networks provide flexibility, mobility, and convenience, allowing devices to connect and communicate without physical cables. Let's dive into the world of wireless technologies!

Section 2: Wireless LAN (WLAN) Concepts

Wireless LANs, or WLANs, are local area networks that utilize wireless communication to connect devices. Understanding WLAN concepts is essential for designing, configuring, and securing wireless networks. Here are some key concepts:

Access Points (APs):

Access points are devices that enable wireless connectivity. They serve as central points for wireless devices to connect to the network. APs transmit and receive wireless signals, allowing communication between wireless devices and the wired network.

SSID (Service Set Identifier):

The SSID is a unique name assigned to a wireless network. Wireless devices use the SSID to identify and connect to a specific WLAN.

Wireless Channels:

Wireless channels divide the available frequency spectrum into smaller bands for communication. Different channels are used to minimize interference and maximize the number of available wireless networks.

Wireless Security:

Securing a wireless network is crucial to protect data and prevent unauthorized access. Common security measures include encryption protocols (e.g., WPA2/WPA3), strong passwords, MAC address filtering, and disabling SSID broadcasting.

Section 3: Wi-Fi Standards

Wi-Fi standards define the specifications and protocols for wireless network communication. Understanding these standards helps ensure compatibility and optimal performance. Here are some Wi-Fi standards:

IEEE 802.11 Standards:

The IEEE 802.11 family of standards provides the foundation for Wi-Fi. Common standards include:

802.11b: Provides data rates up to 11 Mbps in the 2.4 GHz frequency range.

802.11g: Supports data rates up to 54 Mbps in the 2.4 GHz frequency range.

802.11n: Offers increased throughput, MIMO (Multiple Input Multiple Output) technology, and support for both 2.4 GHz and 5 GHz frequency bands.

802.11ac: Provides higher data rates, improved capacity, and support for the 5 GHz frequency band.

802.11ax (Wi-Fi 6): Introduces higher efficiency, increased capacity, and better performance in dense environments.

Wi-Fi Alliance Certifications:

The Wi-Fi Alliance certifies devices for compliance with Wi-Fi standards. Certifications, such as Wi-Fi Certified 6 (based on 802.11ax), ensure interoperability and adherence to industry best practices.

Section 4: Wireless Security and Authentication

Securing wireless networks is essential to protect data and prevent unauthorized access. Here are some wireless security and authentication mechanisms:

WPA/WPA2/WPA3:

Wi-Fi Protected Access (WPA), WPA2, and WPA3 are security protocols that provide encryption and authentication for wireless networks. WPA3 is the latest and most secure standard, offering enhanced protection against security vulnerabilities.

802.1X/EAP (Extensible Authentication Protocol):

802.1X/EAP is an authentication framework that enables secure authentication of wireless clients. It allows for user-based authentication, such as using usernames and passwords or digital certificates.

MAC Address Filtering:

MAC address filtering restricts access to a wireless network based on the MAC addresses of devices. Only devices with approved MAC addresses can connect to the network.

Wireless Intrusion Detection and Prevention Systems (WIDS/WIPS):

WIDS/WIPS monitor wireless networks for unauthorized access, rogue devices, and security threats. They detect and respond to potential security incidents in real-time.

Section 5: Wireless Site Survey

Conducting a wireless site survey is crucial for designing and deploying a reliable wireless network. A site survey helps assess signal strength, identify coverage areas, and mitigate interference. Here's an overview of the site survey process:

Pre-Survey Planning:

Define the objectives, identify deployment locations, and gather information about the physical environment.

Signal Measurements:

Use specialized tools to measure signal strength, signal-to-noise ratio (SNR), and interference levels throughout the coverage area.

Coverage Analysis:

Evaluate signal coverage, identify dead zones or weak signal areas, and determine the optimal placement of access points.

Interference Analysis:

Identify and mitigate sources of interference, such as other wireless networks, Bluetooth devices, or electronic equipment.

Documentation:

Create a detailed report documenting the survey findings, including access point placements, signal coverage maps, and recommended adjustments.

By performing a thorough wireless site survey, you can optimize coverage, minimize interference, and ensure reliable wireless connectivity.

Congratulations on completing Chapter 8! In this chapter, you learned about wireless technologies, including WLAN concepts, Wi-Fi standards, wireless security, and authentication mechanisms. You also explored the importance of wireless site surveys for optimal network performance. In the next chapter, we will delve into network automation and programmability, enabling you to automate network tasks and enhance operational efficiency.

Chapter 9: Network Automation and Programmability

Section 1: Introduction to Network Automation

Welcome to Chapter 9 of our CCNA Exam Prep book! In this chapter, we will explore network automation and programmability, which are key components of modern networking. Automation enables the streamlining of network management tasks, improves operational efficiency, and allows for faster deployment and configuration changes. Let's dive into the world of network automation!

Section 2: Network Automation Benefits and Tools

Network automation offers several benefits, including increased efficiency, reduced human errors, and improved scalability. Here are some key advantages:

Configuration Management:

Automating configuration tasks ensures consistency and accuracy across devices. Changes can be applied simultaneously, reducing manual effort and potential errors.

Network Monitoring and Troubleshooting:

Automation tools can monitor network devices, collect data, and provide proactive alerts for potential issues. Troubleshooting can be expedited with automated diagnostics and remediation.

Provisioning and Deployment:

Automation simplifies the process of deploying new network devices and services. It enables faster provisioning, configuration, and validation, reducing time-to-service for new deployments.

Scalability and Agility:

With automation, network infrastructure can scale efficiently, adapting to changing business needs and reducing the time required to implement changes.

To achieve network automation, various tools and technologies are available, such as Ansible, Puppet, Chef, and network orchestration platforms like Cisco DNA Center.

Section 3: Network Programmability and APIs

Network programmability enables the automation of network tasks through programmable interfaces. APIs (Application Programming Interfaces) provide the means to interact with network devices and services programmatically. Here are some key concepts:

APIs and RESTful APIs:

APIs allow external applications to communicate and interact with network devices. RESTful APIs use the HTTP protocol to exchange data and are widely used in network programmability.

NETCONF (Network Configuration Protocol) and YANG (Yet Another Next Generation):

NETCONF is a network management protocol used for configuration and monitoring of network devices. YANG is a modeling language that provides a standardized way to define the data structure and operations in NETCONF.

Automation Scripts and Programming Languages:

Programming languages like Python, Bash, and PowerShell are commonly used to create automation scripts. These scripts can interact with APIs and automate network tasks.

Section 4: Software-Defined Networking (SDN)

Software-Defined Networking (SDN) is an architectural approach that separates the control plane from the data plane in network devices. Key components of SDN include:

SDN Controller:

The SDN controller is a centralized entity that manages and controls network devices. It provides a single point of control for network programmability and automation.

OpenFlow:

OpenFlow is a protocol used to communicate between the SDN controller and network devices. It allows the controller to instruct switches on how to forward traffic based on the network policies defined.

Network Programmability in SDN:

SDN offers enhanced programmability, allowing for dynamic control and management of network resources through automation and centralized policies.

Section 5: Network Telemetry and Analytics

Network telemetry provides real-time monitoring and collection of network data. Analyzing this data helps identify trends, troubleshoot issues, and make informed decisions. Here are some key components:

Telemetry Data Sources:

Telemetry data can be collected from network devices, interfaces, applications, and protocols. This data provides insights into network performance, utilization, and user experience.

Streaming Telemetry:

Streaming telemetry provides continuous data updates in real-time, enabling proactive monitoring and automation. It offers granular visibility into network conditions and facilitates network troubleshooting.

Network Analytics:

Network analytics involves analyzing telemetry data to gain valuable insights and make data-driven decisions. It can help identify patterns, detect anomalies, and optimize network performance.

By leveraging network telemetry and analytics, organizations can gain valuable insights into their network infrastructure and make informed decisions for performance optimization.

Congratulations on completing Chapter 9! In this chapter, you learned about network automation and programmability, including the benefits of automation, network APIs, software-defined networking (SDN), and network telemetry and analytics. These concepts and tools are crucial for streamlining network management and enhancing operational efficiency. In the next chapter, we will explore network virtualization and software-defined infrastructure, enabling flexible and scalable network architectures.

Chapter 10: Network Virtualization and Software-Defined Infrastructure

Section 1: Introduction to Network Virtualization

Welcome to Chapter 10 of our CCNA Exam Prep book! In this chapter, we will explore network virtualization and software-defined infrastructure, which revolutionize network architectures by providing flexibility, scalability, and simplified management. Network virtualization allows the creation of virtual networks on top of physical infrastructure, while software-defined infrastructure enables centralized control and programmability. Let's dive into the world of network virtualization!

Section 2: Virtual Local Area Networks (VLANs)

Virtual Local Area Networks (VLANs) allow the segmentation of a physical LAN into multiple logical networks. VLANs provide isolation, security, and efficient network resource utilization. Here's what you need to know about VLANs:

VLAN Membership:

Devices within a VLAN can communicate with each other as if they are connected to the same physical LAN, regardless of their physical location. Devices in different VLANs require a router or a layer 3 switch for inter-VLAN communication.

VLAN Tagging:

VLAN tagging is used to identify VLAN membership of Ethernet frames as they traverse through network switches. IEEE 802.1Q is the most common VLAN tagging protocol.

Trunk Links:

Trunk links are connections between switches that carry traffic for multiple VLANs. Trunk links use VLAN tagging to differentiate and segregate VLAN traffic.

Section 3: Virtualization Technologies

Virtualization technologies enable the creation of virtual instances of network resources, such as virtual machines (VMs) and virtual network functions (VNFs). Here are two key virtualization technologies:

Virtual Machines (VMs):

Virtual machines are software-based representations of physical computers. Each VM operates independently and can run its own operating system and applications. Hypervisors, such as VMware ESXi or Microsoft Hyper-V, enable the creation and management of VMs.

Network Function Virtualization (NFV):

Network Function Virtualization decouples network functions, such as firewalls, load balancers, or routers, from dedicated hardware devices. Instead, these functions are virtualized and run as software instances on standard servers. NFV provides flexibility and scalability in deploying network services.

Section 4: Software-Defined Networking (SDN)

Software-Defined Networking (SDN) is an architectural approach that separates the network control plane from the data plane, enabling centralized control and programmability. Here are key components of SDN:

SDN Controller:

The SDN controller is a centralized entity that manages and controls the network. It provides a global view of the

network and translates high-level policies into specific
network configurations.

Southbound and Northbound APIs:

Southbound APIs allow communication between the SDN
controller and network devices. These APIs enable the
controller to instruct network devices on how to forward
traffic. Northbound APIs facilitate communication between
the SDN controller and higher-level applications or services.

Network Programmability:

SDN allows for network programmability, enabling
automation, dynamic traffic control, and rapid deployment of
network services. It simplifies network management and
allows for more flexible and agile network architectures.

Section 5: Network Function Virtualization (NFV) and SDN Integration

NFV and SDN are often deployed together to create more
flexible and efficient network infrastructures. NFV leverages
SDN's centralized control and programmability to orchestrate
and manage virtual network functions. Here's how NFV and
SDN integration works:

Virtual Network Function (VNF):

VNFs are software-based representations of network functions that run on virtualized infrastructure. SDN provides the control and connectivity needed to deploy and manage VNFs dynamically.

NFV Orchestrator:

The NFV Orchestrator is responsible for managing the lifecycle of VNFs. It interacts with the SDN controller to provision and configure the network resources required for VNF deployment.

Service Chaining:

Service chaining involves the sequential traversal of multiple VNFs to provide a complete network service. SDN directs traffic flow through the appropriate VNFs based on service requirements.

Section 6: Network Virtualization and Security

Network virtualization introduces new security considerations. Here are some key security aspects to consider when implementing network virtualization:

Isolation and Segmentation:

Ensure proper isolation between different virtual networks to prevent unauthorized access or data leakage. Use VLANs, virtual firewalls, or other security mechanisms to enforce segmentation.

Virtual Network Monitoring:

Implement network monitoring tools specifically designed for virtualized environments. These tools provide visibility into virtual network traffic, helping detect and respond to security incidents.

Virtual Network Security Policies:

Define and enforce security policies specific to virtual networks. These policies may include access controls, traffic filtering, encryption, and security group configurations.

Hypervisor Security:

Protect the hypervisor environment, as it serves as the foundation for virtualization. Apply security patches, harden configurations, and restrict access to the hypervisor infrastructure.

By understanding the unique security challenges of network virtualization, you can implement robust security measures to protect virtualized environments.

Congratulations on completing Chapter 10! In this chapter, you learned about network virtualization, including VLANs, virtualization technologies such as virtual machines and NFV, and the concepts and components of software-defined networking (SDN). You also explored the integration of NFV and SDN for more flexible network infrastructures and the security considerations in virtualized environments. In the next chapter, we will cover network design principles and best practices, enabling you to design efficient and scalable networks.

Chapter 11: Network Design Principles and Best Practices

Section 1: Introduction to Network Design

Welcome to Chapter 11 of our CCNA Exam Prep book! In this chapter, we will explore network design principles and best practices. Designing a network involves considering various factors, such as scalability, performance, security, and resilience. A well-designed network ensures efficient and reliable communication. Let's dive into the world of network design!

Section 2: Network Design Methodology

Network design follows a systematic approach to ensure a well-planned and effective network architecture. Here's a typical network design methodology:

Gather Requirements:

Understand the business needs, network goals, and technical requirements. Consider factors such as expected traffic volume, application requirements, security requirements, and future growth plans.

Network Topology Design:

Define the network topology based on the requirements. Consider factors such as network size, geographic locations, and connectivity requirements. Common topologies include bus, star, ring, mesh, and hybrid topologies.

Addressing and IP Scheme Design:

Plan the IP addressing scheme, subnetting, and VLAN assignments. Ensure efficient utilization of IP addresses and proper segmentation of network resources.

Network Device Selection:

Select appropriate network devices based on the network requirements. Consider factors such as throughput, scalability, security features, and compatibility with existing infrastructure.

Redundancy and Resilience:

Design for high availability by incorporating redundancy and resilience mechanisms. This may include redundant links, redundant devices, backup power supplies, and failover mechanisms.

Security Considerations:

Integrate security measures into the network design. Consider factors such as firewalls, access control, encryption, network segmentation, and intrusion detection/prevention systems.

Documentation:

Document the network design, including network diagrams, IP addressing plans, device configurations, and security policies. Proper documentation aids in troubleshooting, maintenance, and future modifications.

Section 3: Scalability and Performance Optimization

Designing a network that can scale and perform optimally is crucial. Here are some key considerations for scalability and performance optimization:

Network Segmentation:

Segment the network using VLANs or virtual routing and forwarding (VRF) to isolate traffic and improve performance. This enables better control of broadcast domains and reduces the impact of network congestion.

Bandwidth Planning:

Estimate the required bandwidth based on application requirements, traffic patterns, and future growth projections. Ensure sufficient bandwidth for critical applications and design for scalability.

Quality of Service (QoS):

Implement QoS mechanisms to prioritize network traffic based on application requirements. QoS ensures that critical traffic receives preferential treatment and prevents congestion.

Traffic Engineering:

Optimize network performance by applying traffic engineering techniques. This may involve load balancing, traffic shaping, route optimization, and path selection mechanisms.

Section 4: Network Security Design

Network security is a critical aspect of network design. Consider these key factors when designing for network security:

Perimeter Security:

Implement firewalls, intrusion prevention systems (IPS), and demilitarized zones (DMZs) to protect the network from external threats.

Access Control:

Enforce strong access controls through mechanisms such as authentication, authorization, and accounting (AAA) protocols, role-based access controls (RBAC), and secure management protocols.

Network Segmentation:

Use network segmentation techniques, such as VLANs or virtual private networks (VPNs), to isolate and protect sensitive data and resources.

Data Encryption:

Implement encryption mechanisms, such as IPsec or SSL/TLS, to secure data in transit. Encryption ensures that data remains confidential and protected from eavesdropping.

Section 5: Network Documentation and Change Management

Proper documentation and change management practices are essential for network design and maintenance. Consider the following best practices:

Network Diagrams:

Create detailed network diagrams that depict the network topology, device interconnections, and IP addressing. Update the diagrams regularly to reflect any changes.

Configuration Management:

Maintain accurate records of network device configurations. Implement version control and backup mechanisms to track and restore device configurations.

Change Management:

Establish a change management process to track and control network changes. This includes planning, testing, implementing, and validating changes to minimize disruptions and ensure proper configuration control.

Disaster Recovery Planning:

Develop a comprehensive disaster recovery plan to mitigate the impact of network failures or disruptions. Regularly test the plan and update it as the network evolves.

By following proper network design principles and best practices, you can ensure a reliable, scalable, and secure network infrastructure.

Congratulations on completing Chapter 11! In this chapter, you learned about network design principles and best practices, including network design methodology, scalability and performance optimization, network security design, and network documentation and change management. Applying these principles will help you design efficient and resilient networks. In the next chapter, we will explore network troubleshooting techniques and methodologies to identify and resolve network issues effectively.

Chapter 12: Network Troubleshooting Techniques and Methodologies

Section 1: Introduction to Network Troubleshooting

Welcome to Chapter 12 of our CCNA Exam Prep book! In this chapter, we will explore network troubleshooting techniques and methodologies. Troubleshooting is an essential skill for network administrators, allowing them to identify and resolve network issues efficiently. By understanding troubleshooting methodologies and employing effective techniques, you can ensure smooth network operation. Let's dive into the world of network troubleshooting!

Section 2: Troubleshooting Methodologies

Network troubleshooting follows a systematic approach to identify and resolve issues. Here are two common troubleshooting methodologies:

The OSI Model Approach:

The OSI (Open Systems Interconnection) model divides network functions into seven layers. When troubleshooting, start from the physical layer and work your way up to the application layer. This approach helps narrow down the potential sources of the problem.

The Top-Down Approach:

The top-down approach focuses on the symptoms and starts troubleshooting at the application layer, gradually moving down to the lower layers. It involves analyzing user complaints, testing applications, and examining network services and devices.

Both methodologies provide a structured framework for troubleshooting, allowing you to isolate and resolve network issues effectively.

Section 3: Troubleshooting Tools

Network troubleshooting requires the use of various tools. Here are some common tools used in network troubleshooting:

Ping:

Ping is a basic network utility that tests connectivity by sending ICMP Echo Request packets to a destination IP address. It helps verify if a host is reachable and measures round-trip time (RTT).

Traceroute:

Traceroute is a tool that traces the path packets take from a source to a destination. It shows the network hops and measures the round-trip time for each hop. Traceroute helps identify network latency and routing issues.

Network Analyzers:

Network analyzers, also known as packet sniffers, capture and analyze network traffic. They help troubleshoot network performance, examine network protocols, and detect anomalies or errors.

Cable Testers:

Cable testers check the integrity of network cables. They verify cable continuity, identify open or shorted cables, and detect cable faults or wiring issues.

Port Scanners:

Port scanners are used to scan network devices for open ports and identify services running on those ports. They help identify potential security vulnerabilities or misconfigurations.

Protocol Analyzers:

Protocol analyzers capture and analyze network protocols to understand how data is transmitted and received. They assist in troubleshooting protocol-related issues and analyzing packet-level details.

Section 4: Troubleshooting Common Network Issues

Network issues can arise from various sources, such as misconfigurations, hardware failures, or security threats. Here are some common network issues and troubleshooting techniques:

Connectivity Issues:

Physical Layer: Check cables, connectors, and physical connections for any faults or damages.

Configuration Issues: Verify device configurations, including IP addresses, subnet masks, and default gateways.

Network Addressing: Ensure correct IP addressing, subnetting, and DHCP configurations.

Performance Issues:

Bandwidth Bottlenecks: Identify devices or links causing high network utilization and congestion.

Quality of Service (QoS): Check QoS configurations to ensure proper prioritization of critical traffic.

Network Protocol Issues: Analyze network protocols for misconfigurations or compatibility issues.

Security Incidents:

Firewall Configurations: Verify firewall rules and configurations to ensure proper security measures.

Intrusion Detection Systems (IDS) and Intrusion Prevention Systems (IPS): Monitor and investigate IDS/IPS alerts for potential security breaches.

Malware or Virus Infections: Run anti-malware scans and ensure devices are up to date with security patches.

Section 5: Troubleshooting Remote Network Issues

Troubleshooting remote network issues presents unique challenges. Here are some techniques for troubleshooting remote network problems:

Remote Access:

Use remote access tools, such as VPN (Virtual Private Network) or remote desktop software, to connect to remote devices for troubleshooting.

Troubleshooting Protocols:

Leverage out-of-band management protocols, such as SNMP or SSH, to access and troubleshoot remote devices even if the primary network is inaccessible.

Network Monitoring and Logging:

Implement centralized network monitoring and logging solutions to capture and analyze remote network events and logs.

Collaboration Tools:

Utilize collaboration tools, such as video conferencing or screen-sharing applications, to communicate and troubleshoot with remote users or colleagues.

Section 6: Documentation and Knowledge Base

Maintaining proper documentation and a knowledge base is vital for effective network troubleshooting. Consider the following best practices:

Network Documentation:

Document network topology, device configurations, IP addressing, and changes made to the network. This documentation aids in understanding network architecture and expedites troubleshooting.

Knowledge Base:

Create a knowledge base containing troubleshooting guides, common network issues, and resolutions. This resource can serve as a reference for network administrators and streamline the troubleshooting process.

Collaboration and Communication:

Establish efficient communication channels, such as team chat platforms or ticketing systems, to facilitate collaboration and information sharing among network administrators.

By following effective troubleshooting methodologies, utilizing the right tools, and maintaining proper documentation, you can identify and resolve network issues promptly.

Congratulations on completing Chapter 12! In this chapter, you learned about network troubleshooting techniques and methodologies, including systematic approaches to troubleshooting, common troubleshooting tools, and techniques for addressing network issues. These skills will enable you to diagnose and resolve network problems effectively. In the next chapter, we will explore network monitoring and performance optimization, empowering you to monitor and maintain network performance for optimal operation.

Chapter 13: Network Monitoring and Performance Optimization

Section 1: Introduction to Network Monitoring

Welcome to Chapter 13 of our CCNA Exam Prep book! In this chapter, we will explore network monitoring and performance optimization. Network monitoring involves tracking network performance, identifying issues, and ensuring optimal operation. By effectively monitoring your network, you can proactively detect and resolve problems, resulting in improved performance and user experience. Let's dive into the world of network monitoring!

Section 2: Network Monitoring Tools

Network monitoring tools provide visibility into network performance, traffic patterns, and device health. Here are some commonly used network monitoring tools:

SNMP Monitoring:

Simple Network Management Protocol (SNMP) monitoring allows you to collect data from SNMP-enabled devices, such as routers and switches. SNMP monitoring tools retrieve information such as CPU utilization, interface status, and device health.

Packet Sniffers:

Packet sniffers capture and analyze network traffic, providing insights into protocols, bandwidth usage, and application behavior. Wireshark is a popular packet sniffer tool widely used for network troubleshooting and analysis.

Flow-based Monitoring:

Flow-based monitoring tools, such as NetFlow or sFlow, analyze network traffic flows. They provide detailed information on source and destination IP addresses, ports, protocols, and data volume. Flow data helps identify network bottlenecks and anomalies.

Performance Monitoring:

Performance monitoring tools measure and track network performance metrics, such as response time, throughput, and packet loss. These tools help assess network health, identify performance bottlenecks, and track historical trends.

Section 3: Network Performance Metrics

Monitoring network performance involves tracking various metrics to evaluate the health and efficiency of your network. Here are some key performance metrics:

Latency:

Latency measures the delay between the transmission of a packet and its receipt at the destination. Low latency is crucial for real-time applications like video conferencing or VoIP to ensure smooth communication.

Bandwidth Utilization:

Bandwidth utilization represents the percentage of available bandwidth being used. Monitoring bandwidth utilization helps identify network congestion and plan for capacity upgrades.

Packet Loss:

Packet loss measures the percentage of packets that do not reach their destination. High packet loss can lead to retransmissions, degraded application performance, and network congestion.

Network Response Time:

Network response time measures the time taken for a request to travel from a source to a destination and receive a response. Monitoring response time helps assess application performance and user experience.

Section 4: Alerts and Notifications

Network monitoring tools can generate alerts and notifications based on predefined thresholds or events. These alerts notify network administrators of potential issues or breaches. Consider the following:

Threshold-based Alerts:

Configure thresholds for performance metrics, such as bandwidth utilization or CPU usage. When a threshold is exceeded, the monitoring tool triggers an alert to notify administrators.

Event-based Alerts:

Define specific events or conditions that should trigger an alert. These events could include link failures, high error rates, or security incidents. Event-based alerts help identify critical issues promptly.

Notifications and Escalations:

Configure notifications to be sent via email, SMS, or integration with collaboration tools like Slack or Microsoft Teams. Define escalation procedures to ensure alerts are appropriately addressed if initial notifications are not acknowledged.

Section 5: Network Performance Optimization

Optimizing network performance is crucial for delivering reliable and efficient services. Here are some strategies for network performance optimization:

Quality of Service (QoS):

Implement QoS mechanisms to prioritize critical traffic and ensure sufficient bandwidth for applications with high demands. QoS allows you to control and allocate network resources effectively.

Traffic Engineering:

Optimize traffic flows by load balancing, path selection, and traffic shaping techniques. Traffic engineering helps avoid congestion, reduce latency, and maximize network capacity.

Bandwidth Optimization:

Identify bandwidth-intensive applications or non-essential traffic and apply traffic shaping or rate limiting to optimize bandwidth utilization. This ensures that critical applications receive the necessary bandwidth.

Network Segmentation:

Segment the network using VLANs or virtual routing and forwarding (VRF) to isolate traffic and improve performance. Network segmentation enhances security and reduces the impact of network congestion.

Section 6: Historical Analysis and Capacity Planning

Performing historical analysis and capacity planning helps anticipate future network requirements and proactively address potential issues. Consider the following:

Trend Analysis:

Analyze historical data to identify patterns, trends, and recurring issues. This analysis helps predict future network demands and plan for capacity upgrades or changes.

Capacity Planning:

Estimate network growth and assess resource utilization. Plan for network capacity upgrades, such as additional bandwidth, storage, or processing power, to accommodate future needs.

Forecasting and Predictive Analysis:

Use forecasting techniques and predictive analysis to estimate future network traffic, device utilization, and resource requirements. This helps avoid performance bottlenecks and ensures a smooth user experience.

By implementing effective network monitoring practices, tracking performance metrics, optimizing network performance, and performing capacity planning, you can maintain a reliable and high-performing network.

Congratulations on completing Chapter 13! In this chapter, you learned about network monitoring and performance optimization, including network monitoring tools, performance metrics, alerts and notifications, network performance optimization strategies, and historical analysis for capacity planning. These skills will enable you to proactively monitor and optimize your network for optimal performance. In the next chapter, we will explore network security best practices, equipping you with the knowledge to protect your network from potential threats.

Chapter 14: Network Security Best Practices

Section 1: Introduction to Network Security

Welcome to Chapter 14 of our CCNA Exam Prep book! In this chapter, we will explore network security best practices. Network security is paramount in protecting your network from unauthorized access, data breaches, and other security threats. By implementing effective security measures and following industry best practices, you can safeguard your network and ensure the confidentiality, integrity, and availability of your data. Let's dive into the world of network security!

Section 2: Network Security Fundamentals

Before diving into specific security measures, let's establish some fundamental concepts:

Defense-in-Depth:

Defense-in-depth is a layered security approach that employs multiple security measures at different levels. By having multiple layers of defense, you create a more robust and comprehensive security posture.

Confidentiality, Integrity, and Availability (CIA):

CIA is the triad of information security. It ensures that data is kept confidential, remains unaltered (integrity), and is accessible to authorized users when needed (availability).

Risk Assessment:

Conducting regular risk assessments helps identify potential vulnerabilities and threats. It enables you to prioritize security measures based on the identified risks.

Section 3: Access Control and Authentication

Access control and authentication mechanisms ensure that only authorized individuals or devices can access network resources. Consider the following best practices:

User Access Control:

Implement user access controls, such as strong passwords or multi-factor authentication (MFA). Enforce password complexity rules, regular password changes, and account lockout policies.

Network Device Access Control:

Secure network device access by using secure management protocols (SSH, HTTPS), strong passwords, and role-based access control (RBAC) to restrict administrative privileges.

Network Segmentation:

Segment the network into smaller, isolated segments using VLANs or virtual private networks (VPNs). This helps restrict access to sensitive resources and limits the spread of potential security breaches.

Section 4: Firewalls and Intrusion Prevention Systems

Firewalls and intrusion prevention systems (IPS) play a crucial role in network security. Consider the following best practices:

Perimeter Firewalls:

Deploy perimeter firewalls to protect the network from external threats. Configure firewall rules to allow only necessary traffic and block unauthorized access attempts.

Internal Firewalls:

Implement internal firewalls to protect critical internal segments, such as servers or databases, from lateral movement and unauthorized access within the network.

Intrusion Prevention Systems (IPS):

Deploy IPS devices to detect and prevent network-based attacks. IPS devices monitor network traffic and can block malicious traffic based on predefined rules or behavioral analysis.

Section 5: Network Monitoring and Logging

Network monitoring and logging are essential for detecting security incidents and analyzing network behavior. Consider the following best practices:

Network Traffic Monitoring:

Use network monitoring tools to capture and analyze network traffic. Monitor for anomalies, unusual patterns, or suspicious activities that may indicate a security breach.

Event Logging:

Enable event logging on network devices and security appliances. Centralize logs in a secure log management system for analysis and detection of security incidents.

Security Information and Event Management (SIEM):

Implement a SIEM system to aggregate and correlate log data from various network devices and security tools. SIEM provides real-time analysis and alerts for potential security incidents.

Section 6: Security Policies and Awareness

Establishing security policies and raising security awareness among users are critical components of network security. Consider the following best practices:

Security Policies:

Develop comprehensive security policies that outline acceptable use, password requirements, incident response procedures, and other security guidelines. Regularly review and update these policies.

User Education and Awareness:

Educate users about common security threats, social engineering techniques, and best practices. Conduct regular security awareness training to ensure users understand their role in maintaining network security.

Incident Response:

Establish an incident response plan that defines the steps to be taken in the event of a security incident. Ensure all stakeholders are aware of their roles and responsibilities during an incident.

Section 7: Regular Updates and Patch Management

Keeping network devices and software up to date with the latest patches and security updates is crucial for addressing known vulnerabilities. Consider the following best practices:

Patch Management:

Implement a patch management process to identify, test, and deploy security patches and updates for network devices, operating systems, and applications in a timely manner.

Firmware Upgrades:

Regularly update firmware on network devices to address security vulnerabilities and benefit from new features and bug fixes provided by the manufacturer.

Vulnerability Assessments and Penetration Testing:

Perform regular vulnerability assessments and penetration testing to identify weaknesses and validate the effectiveness of security controls. Address identified vulnerabilities promptly.

By implementing these network security best practices, you can establish a strong security posture and protect your network from potential threats.

Congratulations on completing Chapter 14! In this chapter, you learned about network security best practices, including access control, authentication, firewalls, intrusion prevention systems, network monitoring and logging, security policies and awareness, and regular updates and patch management. By following these practices, you can ensure a secure network environment. In the next chapter, we will explore emerging technologies and trends in networking, keeping you up to date with the latest advancements in the field.

Chapter 15: Emerging Technologies and Trends in Networking

Section 1: Introduction to Emerging Technologies

Welcome to Chapter 15 of our CCNA Exam Prep book! In this chapter, we will explore emerging technologies and trends in networking. The field of networking is constantly evolving, with new technologies and trends shaping the future of network infrastructure. By staying informed about these emerging advancements, you can adapt and prepare for the networking landscape of tomorrow. Let's dive into the world of emerging technologies in networking!

Section 2: Software-Defined Networking (SDN)

Software-Defined Networking (SDN) continues to be a significant trend in networking. SDN separates the control plane from the data plane, allowing for centralized control and programmability. Consider the following aspects of SDN:

SDN Controllers:

SDN controllers provide a centralized point of control for network devices. They enable dynamic network management, automation, and orchestration.

Network Programmability:

SDN allows for network programmability through APIs and software-defined interfaces. This enables automation, rapid service deployment, and flexible network configuration.

Intent-Based Networking (IBN):

IBN builds upon the principles of SDN by leveraging machine learning and artificial intelligence (AI) to align network operations with business intent. It aims to automate network operations and optimize network performance based on desired outcomes.

Section 3: Network Function Virtualization (NFV)

Network Function Virtualization (NFV) is another emerging trend that virtualizes network functions, such as firewalls, load balancers, or routers. Consider the following aspects of NFV:

Virtual Network Functions (VNFs):

VNFs are software-based instances of network functions that run on virtualized infrastructure. They provide flexibility, scalability, and cost-effectiveness compared to traditional dedicated hardware appliances.

NFV Infrastructure (NFVI):

NFVI refers to the virtualized infrastructure that supports the deployment and operation of VNFs. It includes compute, storage, and networking resources required to run VNFs.

Orchestration and Management:

NFV orchestration involves managing the lifecycle of VNFs, including provisioning, scaling, and monitoring. It ensures efficient resource utilization and seamless service delivery.

Section 4: Internet of Things (IoT)

The Internet of Things (IoT) is the network of interconnected devices, sensors, and objects that communicate and exchange data. Consider the following aspects of IoT:

Device Proliferation:

IoT devices are rapidly proliferating, connecting various devices and enabling data collection and automation in diverse industries, such as healthcare, manufacturing, and transportation.

Connectivity and Networking Challenges:

IoT devices require reliable connectivity options, such as Wi-Fi, cellular, or low-power wide-area networks (LPWAN). Network architectures must accommodate the increasing number of IoT devices and handle the associated data traffic.

Security Considerations:

Securing IoT devices and data is a critical challenge. IoT devices often have limited processing power and may lack built-in security features. Implementing strong security measures, such as device authentication, data encryption, and network segmentation, is essential.

Section 5: 5G and Network Convergence

The advent of 5G technology brings higher speeds, lower latency, and increased capacity, enabling new possibilities for networking. Consider the following aspects of 5G and network convergence:

Enhanced Mobile Broadband (eMBB):

5G enables faster data speeds, providing an enhanced user experience for bandwidth-intensive applications like video streaming, virtual reality, and augmented reality.

Ultra-Reliable Low-Latency Communication (URLLC):

URLLC supports applications with stringent requirements for reliability and low latency, such as autonomous vehicles, industrial automation, and remote surgery.

Massive Machine-Type Communication (mMTC):

mMTC facilitates the connectivity of a vast number of IoT devices, allowing for efficient data exchange and enabling applications like smart cities and industrial IoT.

Network Convergence:

With 5G, there is an increasing convergence of wired and wireless networks. Fiber-optic networks, Wi-Fi 6, and 5G networks work together to provide seamless connectivity and enhanced user experiences.

Section 6: Cloud Computing and Network Virtualization

Cloud computing and network virtualization are transforming the way networks are designed, deployed, and managed. Consider the following aspects:

Infrastructure as a Service (IaaS):

IaaS provides virtualized computing resources, storage, and networking capabilities on-demand. It enables organizations to scale their network infrastructure based on their needs.

Network Virtualization in the Cloud:

Virtualized networks in the cloud, often referred to as virtual private clouds (VPCs), allow organizations to create isolated networks with customized configurations and security settings.

Cloud-based Network Services:

Cloud-based network services, such as cloud-based firewalls, load balancers, and virtual private networks (VPNs), offer scalable and cost-effective solutions for network security and connectivity.

Section 7: Artificial Intelligence (AI) and Machine Learning (ML) in Networking

AI and ML are increasingly being applied in networking to optimize operations, improve security, and enhance performance. Consider the following applications:

Network Analytics:

AI and ML algorithms analyze network data to identify patterns, anomalies, and potential security threats. They provide insights into network performance, capacity planning, and optimization.

Network Automation:

AI and ML algorithms enable intelligent automation of network tasks, such as configuration management, fault detection, and predictive maintenance. This improves operational efficiency and reduces human error.

Security Threat Detection:

AI and ML techniques enhance security by detecting and mitigating network threats in real-time. They identify malicious activities, anomalous behavior, and potential vulnerabilities.

By keeping abreast of emerging technologies and trends in networking, you can stay ahead of the curve and leverage these advancements to build more efficient, secure, and scalable networks.

Congratulations on completing Chapter 15! In this chapter, you learned about emerging technologies and trends in networking, including Software-Defined Networking (SDN), Network Function Virtualization (NFV), the Internet of Things (IoT), 5G and network convergence, cloud computing and network virtualization, and the application of Artificial Intelligence (AI) and Machine Learning (ML) in networking. These advancements shape the future of networking and offer exciting possibilities. In the next chapter, we will review key concepts and provide exam preparation tips for the CCNA certification.

Chapter 16: CCNA Exam Preparation and Exam Tips

Section 1: Introduction to CCNA Exam Preparation

Welcome to Chapter 16 of our CCNA Exam Prep book! In this chapter, we will focus on preparing for the CCNA certification exam. The Cisco Certified Network Associate (CCNA) certification validates your knowledge and skills in networking fundamentals, network access, IP connectivity, IP services, security fundamentals, automation, and programmability. This chapter will provide you with exam preparation tips, study resources, and strategies to help you succeed in your CCNA journey. Let's get started!

Section 2: Understanding the CCNA Exam

To effectively prepare for the CCNA exam, it is essential to understand its structure, format, and objectives. Consider the following aspects:

Exam Structure:

The CCNA exam typically consists of multiple-choice questions, drag-and-drop questions, and simulations.

Familiarize yourself with the exam structure to understand the types of questions you will encounter.

Exam Topics:

Review the official exam blueprint provided by Cisco. It outlines the specific topics and subtopics that will be covered in the exam. Use the blueprint as a study guide to ensure you cover all the necessary content.

Exam Duration and Passing Score:

Understand the exam duration and passing score requirements. This will help you manage your time during the exam and set appropriate study goals.

Section 3: Study Resources

Having access to quality study resources is crucial for exam preparation. Consider the following resources:

Official Cisco Study Materials:

Refer to Cisco's official study materials, such as the Cisco Press books or online resources provided by Cisco. These resources are designed to cover the exam objectives comprehensively.

Online Learning Platforms:

Utilize online learning platforms that offer CCNA courses and practice exams. These platforms provide structured learning paths, video tutorials, practice questions, and performance tracking.

CCNA Study Guides:

Explore third-party study guides that provide in-depth coverage of CCNA exam topics. Look for reputable publishers with positive reviews to ensure the accuracy and relevance of the content.

Practice Exams and Sample Questions:

Take advantage of practice exams and sample questions to assess your knowledge and familiarize yourself with the exam format. These resources help you identify areas that require further study and build exam confidence.

Section 4: Study Strategies

Developing effective study strategies can optimize your preparation for the CCNA exam. Consider the following strategies:

Create a Study Plan:

Develop a study plan that outlines your study schedule, topics to cover, and milestones to achieve. Breaking down the content into manageable portions helps you stay organized and focused.

Hands-On Practice:

Gain practical experience by setting up a lab environment or using network simulation tools. Hands-on practice reinforces theoretical concepts and improves your understanding of network operations.

Review and Reinforce:

Regularly review previously covered topics to reinforce your knowledge. Spaced repetition, where you revisit the material at increasing intervals, enhances long-term retention.

Join Study Groups:

Engage with other CCNA candidates by joining study groups or online forums. Collaborating with peers allows you to discuss concepts, clarify doubts, and learn from their experiences.

Section 5: Exam Day Tips

On the day of the CCNA exam, it is essential to be well-prepared and manage your time effectively. Consider the following tips:

Get a Good Night's Sleep:

Ensure you get adequate rest the night before the exam. A well-rested mind performs better and helps you stay focused during the exam.

Read the Questions Carefully:

Take your time to read each question carefully and understand what is being asked. Pay attention to keywords and any additional instructions provided.

Manage Your Time:

The CCNA exam has a time limit, so manage your time wisely. Answer the questions you know well first and mark the ones you're unsure of for review later.

Review Your Answers:

If time permits, review your answers before submitting the exam. Check for any errors or missed questions. Use this time to make any necessary corrections.

Section 6: Exam Retake Strategy

In case you don't pass the CCNA exam on your first attempt, it's important to have a retake strategy. Consider the following steps:

Analyze Your Performance:

Review your exam score report to understand your strengths and weaknesses. Identify areas that need improvement and focus your study efforts accordingly.

Revisit Study Materials:

Refer back to the study resources you used during your initial preparation. Review the topics you struggled with and reinforce your understanding.

Practice Exams:

Take additional practice exams to simulate the exam environment and identify any gaps in your knowledge. Use these practice exams to refine your exam-taking skills.

Seek Additional Support:

Consider seeking additional support, such as online forums, study groups, or tutoring, to gain insights and perspectives from others who have successfully passed the CCNA exam.

By following these exam preparation tips, leveraging study resources effectively, and adopting study strategies, you can increase your chances of success in the CCNA certification exam.

Congratulations on completing Chapter 16! In this chapter, you learned about CCNA exam preparation, including understanding the exam structure and objectives, utilizing study resources, developing study strategies, exam day tips, and retake strategies. By applying these strategies and dedicating sufficient time and effort to your preparation, you can confidently approach the CCNA exam. Good luck on your journey towards becoming a Cisco Certified Network Associate!

Chapter 17: Advanced Networking Concepts

Section 1: Introduction to Advanced Networking Concepts

Welcome to Chapter 17 of our CCNA Exam Prep book! In this chapter, we will delve into advanced networking concepts that build upon the foundational knowledge covered in earlier chapters. Understanding these advanced concepts will further enhance your expertise in networking and help you excel in more complex networking environments. Let's explore these advanced networking concepts!

Section 2: Virtual Private Networks (VPNs)

Virtual Private Networks (VPNs) provide secure, encrypted connections over public networks, allowing users to access private networks remotely. Consider the following aspects of VPNs:

VPN Types:

Explore different types of VPNs, such as site-to-site VPNs and remote access VPNs. Understand their architectures, protocols, and deployment scenarios.

VPN Encryption and Authentication:

Learn about encryption algorithms, such as IPsec and SSL/TLS, used to secure VPN connections. Understand authentication methods, including pre-shared keys and digital certificates.

VPN Deployment:

Understand the process of deploying VPNs, including configuring VPN endpoints, establishing tunnels, and managing VPN connections. Explore different VPN technologies and their respective configurations.

Section 3: Network Address Translation (NAT)

Network Address Translation (NAT) is a technique used to map private IP addresses to public IP addresses, allowing devices on a private network to access the Internet. Consider the following aspects of NAT:

NAT Types:

Learn about the different types of NAT, including Static NAT, Dynamic NAT, and Network Address and Port Translation (NAPT). Understand their purposes and implementation methods.

NAT Configuration:

Explore how to configure NAT on routers or firewalls, including defining NAT translation rules, configuring port forwarding, and troubleshooting NAT-related issues.

NAT Overload (PAT):

Understand how Port Address Translation (PAT) or NAT Overload enables multiple devices to share a single public IP address by using unique port numbers.

Section 4: Quality of Service (QoS)

Quality of Service (QoS) ensures that certain network traffic receives priority treatment, allowing for optimized performance and resource allocation. Consider the following aspects of QoS:

QoS Mechanisms:

Learn about QoS mechanisms, such as traffic classification, congestion management, traffic shaping, and prioritization techniques like Differentiated Services (DiffServ) and Integrated Services (IntServ).

QoS Configuration:

Explore how to configure QoS policies on network devices, including marking traffic, setting up traffic queues, and defining policies for bandwidth allocation and priority handling.

QoS Best Practices:

Understand QoS best practices for different types of network traffic, such as voice and video, and how to ensure optimal performance for critical applications.

Section 5: Wireless Networking

Wireless networking has become pervasive, offering flexibility and mobility in network connectivity. Consider the following aspects of wireless networking:

Wireless Standards and Technologies:

Explore wireless networking standards, such as IEEE 802.11 (Wi-Fi), and their variants, including 802.11ac (Wi-Fi 5) and 802.11ax (Wi-Fi 6). Understand the features, performance, and compatibility of these standards.

Wireless Security:

Learn about wireless security mechanisms, such as Wi-Fi Protected Access (WPA/WPA2) and the latest WPA3, and understand the importance of strong encryption, authentication, and access control in wireless networks.

Wireless Site Survey:

Understand the importance of conducting a wireless site survey to assess signal coverage, interference, and signal strength. Learn about tools and techniques used for site surveys to optimize wireless network performance.

Section 6: Network Virtualization

Network virtualization allows for the creation of virtual networks that are independent of physical network infrastructure, enabling increased flexibility and scalability. Consider the following aspects of network virtualization:

Virtual LANs (VLANs):

Explore VLANs and their benefits, including the ability to logically segment a network, enhance security, and improve traffic management. Learn about VLAN configuration and management.

Virtual Routing and Forwarding (VRF):

Understand VRF, a technique used to create multiple virtual routing tables within a single physical router. Learn about VRF configuration and how it enables network segmentation and isolation.

Network Overlay Technologies:

Explore network overlay technologies, such as Virtual Extensible LAN (VXLAN) and Generic Routing Encapsulation (GRE), used to create virtual network overlays over an existing physical network.

Section 7: Network Automation and Programmability

Network automation and programmability are transforming the way networks are managed, enabling efficient and scalable network operations. Consider the following aspects:

Network Automation Tools:

Learn about network automation tools, such as Ansible, Puppet, or Python scripting, and how they can be used to automate network configurations, deployments, and monitoring.

Software-Defined Networking (SDN):

Build upon your understanding of SDN from earlier chapters and explore advanced SDN concepts, such as network programmability, SDN controllers, and software-defined overlays.

Network APIs:

Understand the role of Application Programming Interfaces (APIs) in network automation and programmability. Explore different types of APIs, such as REST APIs and NETCONF/YANG, and how they facilitate interaction with network devices.

By mastering these advanced networking concepts, you will be well-equipped to tackle complex networking challenges and excel in your career as a network professional.

Congratulations on completing Chapter 17! In this chapter, you explored advanced networking concepts, including Virtual Private Networks (VPNs), Network Address Translation (NAT), Quality of Service (QoS), wireless networking, network virtualization, and network automation and programmability. These concepts will enhance your knowledge and skills in networking, empowering you to tackle more complex networking environments. In the next chapter, we will provide a summary and final exam preparation tips to help you succeed in the CCNA certification exam.

Chapter 18: CCNA Exam Summary and Final Exam Preparation

Section 1: CCNA Exam Summary

Welcome to Chapter 18, the final chapter of our CCNA Exam Prep book! In this chapter, we will provide a summary of the key concepts covered throughout the book and offer final exam preparation tips. This chapter will help you consolidate your knowledge and prepare for the CCNA certification exam. Let's review the key topics and provide you with the tools to succeed!

Section 2: Exam Objectives Recap

Let's recap the main exam objectives covered in this book:

Networking Fundamentals:

Understand networking concepts, OSI and TCP/IP models, Ethernet, IP addressing, and subnetting.

Network Access:

Explore Ethernet LANs, VLANs, trunking, and basic switch configuration.

IP Connectivity:

Learn about IP routing, static and dynamic routing protocols, inter-VLAN routing, and IPv6 addressing.

IP Services:

Understand Network Address Translation (NAT), Dynamic Host Configuration Protocol (DHCP), and Network Time Protocol (NTP).

Security Fundamentals:

Explore security concepts, Access Control Lists (ACLs), secure network management, and device hardening.

Automation and Programmability:

Learn about network automation, infrastructure as code, REST APIs, and the basics of Python scripting.

Section 3: Exam Preparation Tips

To help you excel in the CCNA certification exam, consider the following exam preparation tips:

Review and Reinforce:

Review the key topics covered in each chapter, focusing on areas where you feel less confident. Reinforce your understanding by practicing with sample questions and scenarios.

Hands-On Practice:

Take advantage of hands-on practice to gain practical experience. Set up a lab environment or use network simulation tools to configure devices, troubleshoot issues, and reinforce your knowledge.

Practice Exams:

Take practice exams to familiarize yourself with the exam format and assess your readiness. Identify areas where you need improvement and revisit those topics for further study.

Time Management:

Develop effective time management strategies for the exam. Practice answering questions within the allotted time to ensure you can complete the exam within the time constraints.

Exam Objectives Alignment:

Align your study plan with the official exam objectives provided by Cisco. Ensure you have covered all the required topics and feel confident in your understanding of each objective.

Seek Clarification:

If you come across any ambiguous or unclear concepts, seek clarification through online forums, study groups, or additional study resources. Clearing any doubts will enhance your confidence.

Section 4: Exam-Day Tips

On the day of the CCNA exam, follow these tips to perform your best:

Arrive Early:

Plan to arrive at the exam center early to allow time for check-in procedures. This will help you start the exam with a calm and focused mindset.

Read Carefully:

Read each question carefully, paying attention to keywords and any additional instructions provided. Make sure you fully understand what is being asked before selecting your answer.

Eliminate Options:

If you are unsure of the correct answer, try to eliminate obviously incorrect options. Narrowing down the choices can increase your chances of selecting the correct answer.

Manage Your Time:

Manage your time effectively during the exam. Answer the questions you know well first and mark the ones you're unsure of for review later. Keep an eye on the time to ensure you can complete all the questions.

Stay Calm and Confident:

Maintain a calm and confident mindset throughout the exam. Trust in your preparation and rely on your knowledge and problem-solving skills to tackle the questions.

Section 5: Exam Retake Strategy (If Needed)

If you don't pass the CCNA exam on your first attempt, don't get discouraged. Consider the following steps for your exam retake strategy:

Analyze Your Performance:

Review your exam score report to identify areas where you performed well and areas that require improvement. Focus your study efforts on the weaker areas.

Review and Reinforce:

Revisit study materials and resources to strengthen your understanding of the concepts that need improvement. Take additional practice exams to assess your progress.

Seek Additional Support:

Engage with online forums, study groups, or tutoring to gain insights and perspectives from others who have successfully passed the CCNA exam. Utilize their guidance to enhance your preparation.

Adjust Your Study Plan:

Adjust your study plan based on the feedback received from your exam performance. Focus on the specific topics or objectives where you need improvement, and allocate more time for those areas.

Section 6: Congratulations on Completing the Book!

Congratulations on completing our CCNA Exam Prep book! By studying the concepts covered in this book, leveraging practice exams, and following the exam preparation tips, you are well-equipped to succeed in the CCNA certification exam.

Remember to stay confident, maintain a positive mindset, and trust in your preparation. The CCNA certification is a valuable achievement that will open doors to new opportunities in the field of networking.

Best of luck on your exam, and we hope this book has provided you with the knowledge and skills needed to excel in your CCNA journey.